The Magic School Bus

PRESENTS

Insects

Scholastic Inc.

Photos ©: Alamy Images: 3 bottom, 25 (Arcangelo Manoni), 24 bottom right (Erik Karits), 1 (Renato Granieri); Corbis Images: 22 (Stephen Dalton/Minden Pictures), 28 top right (Tim Zurowski/All Canada Photos), 6 (Willi Rolfes/NiS/Minden Pictures); Dreamstime: cover top left (Ambientideas), 18 top left (Dario Lo Presti), 7 center (Denis Nikitin), 28 bottom right (Igos), 29 top right (Liewwk), 9 (Musat Christian), 18 bottom (Natursports), 28 bottom left (Orionmystery), 19 (Sarah2), 4 –5 (Shuyan Zhang), 3 top, 7 bottom left (Skynetphoto); Getty Images: 20, 21 top right (Adegsm), 14 –15 (Gail Shumway), 30 (Mint Images – Frans Lanting), 21 bottom left (Nick Tsiatinis), 13 bottom right (Rodger Jackman); Nature Picture Library: 7 bottom right (Alex Hyde), 24 top left (Jan Hamrsky), 28 top left (Jane Burton), 10 –11, 29 bottom left (Kim Taylor), 26 –27 (Nature Production), 8 top left (Nick Garbutt), 16 (Philippe Clement), 23 right (Premaphotos), 8 bottom right (Steven David Miller), 31 left (William Osborn); Nikola Rahmé: 29 bottom right; Science Source/Paul Whitten: 12, Shutterstock, Inc./Andrey Pavlov: cover bottom center; Superstock, Inc.: 4 top left, 23 left (Biosphoto), 10 top left (Chris Mattison), 13 bottom left, 14 top left, 29 top left (Minden Pictures); Thinkstock: cover bottom right (Cameramannz), cover background (KrivosheevV), 3 center, 17 bottom right (mady70), 17 bottom left (SaraBerdon), cover bottom left (Valengilda), 26 top left (venemama); USDA/Stephen Ausmus: 31 right.

ISBN 978-0-545-68587-0

Produced by Potomac Global Media, LLC

Published by Scholastic Inc., 557 Broadway, New York, NY 10012.

12 11 10 9 8 7   18 19/0

Cover design by Paul Banks
Interior design by Carol Farrar Norton
Photo research by Sharon Southren

Printed in the U.S.A.   40
First printing, January 2015

Contents

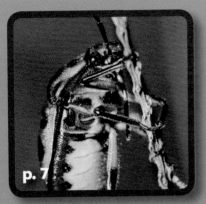

p. 7

p. 17

p. 25

What Is an Insect?

Insects are the only animals that don't have backbones that can fly. These mayflies have four wings, but some insects have just two wings.

Name an insect," said Ms. Frizzle. "Beetle!" shouted Arnold. "A butterfly!" shouted Keesha. "You're both right," said the Friz. "Insects have three pairs of legs, wings, and no backbones. Let's go meet some."

Thorax
The thorax is in the middle of the body.

Head
The eyes, mouth, and antennae are in the head.

To find out all about insects, let's shrink down to their size.

BUGGING OUT!

4

Abdomen

An insect's abdomen is usually soft. This tiger beetle's abdomen is out of sight, beneath its wings.

Miracle spiracles!

How do insects breathe?
by Wanda

All animals need oxygen to survive. They use it to turn food into the energy that powers their bodies. There is oxygen in air and in water. A large animal, like a human, gets its oxygen by breathing air into the lungs.

But insects do not have lungs. Instead, their bodies are covered in tiny holes called spiracles. Air comes in through these openings, and then it flows to all parts of their bodies.

Tiger beetles have long legs for running. They run faster than any other insect.

Frizzle Fact

Around two-thirds of all animal species on Earth are insects. So far, scientists have named nearly one million different types of insects.

Tough Beetles

Male stag beetles appear to have long "horns." In fact, these horns are part of the mouth. Instead of using them to feed, the stag beetle uses them as weapons when fighting over females.

The winner is the one who knocks the other beetle off the branch.

Frizzle Fact

Diving beetles look for new places to swim by flying around during a full moon. If a beetle spots the moon's reflection in a pond, it knows it's found a place to swim.

There are more types of beetles than any other kind of insect. They include ladybugs and fireflies. Beetles have rounded bodies covered in tough armor. They live in all sorts of places. Some swim in ponds, while others live on top of sand dunes.

Winging it!

Can beetles fly?
by Dorothy Ann

Most beetles can fly. They keep their wings safe beneath tough covers on their backs. Like most flying insects, beetles have four wings. However, they only use the delicate hind pair for flying. The front pair is the tough cover.

When it's time to fly, the beetle folds the covers out of the way, and the flying wings go to work. Even large beetles like the Titan, which is a massive 6.5 inches (16.5 centimeters) long, can fly—although it does not go very fast.

Jewel beetles have brightly colored bodies that shimmer in the sunlight.

Some baby beetles are called grubs. They don't look like adult beetles; they look more like worms.

This is a giraffe weevil. Male giraffe weevils have long necks. They use them for fighting and showing off to females.

Beautiful Butterflies

This is a Saturn moth. Moths usually fly at nighttime. They're less brightly colored than butterflies.

Butterflies are easy to see as they flutter around flowers on a sunny day. Butterflies and moths belong to the same group of insects. Both have four wings, but the front and back wings on each side lock together and work like one large wing.

Butterfly Body

Glad I don't taste things with my feet!

Tasting food

A butterfly's feet have taste detectors. The butterfly knows if something is good to eat just by standing on it.

Eyes and antennae

Butterflies have big eyes for spotting flowers. They use antennae to smell, feel, and taste.

Bright colors

Wing patterns are created by tiny plates, or scales, layered on the wings — a bit like tiles on a roof.

Butterflies feed mostly on nectar from wildflowers. They also drink plant sap and the juice of rotting fruits.

Feeding tube

A butterfly sucks nectar through a long tube-shaped mouthpart called a proboscis. When it is not in use, the proboscis coils up under the head.

Massive makeover!

The life cycle of a butterfly
by Carlos

A butterfly starts life as a caterpillar, which hatches from an egg. The caterpillar grows very fast and soon becomes a motionless pupa, hanging from a branch. Inside, the caterpillar changes. When the pupa opens, a butterfly flies away.

Egg

Caterpillar

Butterfly

Pupa

Hopping Crickets

This spiny katydid is a relative of the cricket. It is named for its call, which goes "Katy did, Katy didn't!"

Crickets and grasshoppers are noisy insects. They communicate by making loud, clicking sounds. Crickets call to each other by rubbing rough sections of their wings together. Grasshoppers rub their wings and legs together.

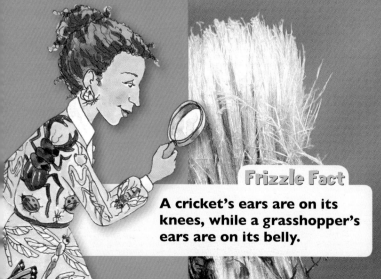

Frizzle Fact

A cricket's ears are on its knees, while a grasshopper's ears are on its belly.

Stormin' swarm!

All about locusts
by Phoebe

Some grasshoppers breed rapidly when there is a lot of food around. This can happen in warm, dry parts of the world after a drought, when food has been scarce. Grasshoppers crowd together, eating whatever they can find. That's what starts a swarm. When they swarm, the grasshoppers develop into locusts. They form a huge cloud and fly around. More and more locusts join until eventually the swarm contains millions of insects. When they all eat at once, they can completely destroy farmers' crops.

Crickets have long, thin antennae. Grasshoppers and locusts have short, thick ones.

Crickets use their long back legs to hop forward. Adult crickets like this one can also fly, but younger ones, called nymphs, have no wings and can only jump.

True Bugs

A cicada spends most of its life as a wingless nymph, tunneling through the ground and sucking sap from the roots of plants. Adult cicadas come aboveground to find mates.

Frizzle Fact

A scale bug protects itself by growing a shield of wax over its body. People collect the wax and use it in wood polish.

Insects and other creepy-crawlies are often called bugs. But bugs are actually just one type of insect, including cicadas, aphids, and water striders. Bugs look a lot like beetles, but they have sucking mouthparts. Unlike beetles, you can usually see the tips of their wings sticking out at the back.

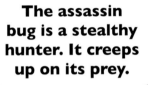

Hungry bugs!

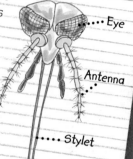

How do bugs eat?
by Ralphie

A true bug has a long, needle-shaped mouthpart, called a stylet, that it uses to suck up liquid food. Most bugs drink sap, a liquid inside plant stems and roots. Sap is not a very good source of food. It's mostly water, with a little bit of sugar. So bugs spend a lot of time feeding.

····· Eye

Antenna
····

····· Stylet

The assassin bug is a stealthy hunter. It creeps up on its prey.

This assassin bug sticks its long, needle-sharp mouthpart into prey — and sucks them dry!

This animal is called a water scorpion, but it's actually a type of bug. The long, spiked tail is not a stinger, but a breathing tube that pokes out of the water.

Army of Ants

Ants live and work as a team to support a queen ant. All the other ants in the nest are called workers. Some build the nest—normally a network of tunnels and chambers underground. Others fight off attackers. The oldest workers collect food from outside the nest.

The queen ant lays eggs, and her workers look after the young ants that hatch. They keep them clean and give them food.

These ants left a trail of scent so they could find their way back to their nest.

Frizzle Fact

Ants cannot swim. When a colony needs to cross a river, the workers cling to one another, making a raft to carry the queen and her eggs across.

Leaf-cutter ants collect bits of leaf. They use them to grow fungus gardens back inside the nest. Then the ants eat the fungus.

An ant can carry many times its own weight.

Girl power!

How do ant colonies work?
by Keesha

All worker ants are female. They are the daughters of the queen, who lays most of the eggs in a colony. Some workers lay eggs to produce male ants. The workers also look after their baby sisters, who will become workers once they are old enough.

Every year, a number of baby ants are given more food and grow into winged ants, both male and female. They fly away to mate. One of them—a new queen—sets up a colony of her own.

Bees and Wasps

This nest is home to hundreds of wasps.

Frizzle Fact
The giant Asian hornet is the largest in the world. A sting from its ¼-inch (6-millimeter) long stinger can be deadly.

The wings of these paper wasps from Costa Rica look purple in the light.

Bees and wasps are related to ants, and many of them live in colonies, supporting a queen. Their bodies have yellow and black stripes—a warning that these insects sting. Many wasps and bees hunt for other insects, which they bring back to their nests and feed to their young.

Yummy honey!

Why do bees make honey?
by Tim

Honey is the honeybee's food. All the bees, young and old, eat it. To make honey, worker bees put the nectar and a bit of pollen they have collected into a chamber in the honeycomb. They fan the liquid so it dries into a thick, sweet goo—honey. The bees store the honey to use as food in winter, when there are fewer flowers. They make so much that humans can have some, too.

Honeybee Worker

Nectar supply
The honeybee sucks up nectar from flowers and stores it in a pouch in its throat.

Pollen basket
A bee collects pollen from a flower and carries it back to the nest in balls stuck to its back legs.

Inside a beehive is the honeycomb—a series of chambers used to store food. The honeycomb also holds young bees as they grow.

Acrobatic Fliers

Ouch! A lot of different flies bite people!

Flies are a group of fast-flying insects that have only two proper wings. They include houseflies and mosquitoes. Flies are very acrobatic creatures—they can fly upside down, do somersaults, and even go backward.

Houseflies start out as maggots. They have no legs and do nothing but eat.

Mosquitoes are small flies that suck blood through a victim's skin.

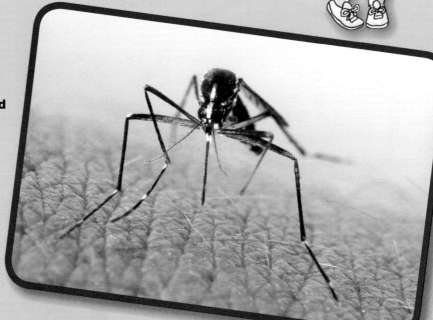

Frizzle Fact

Bites from mosquitoes can spread dangerous diseases, such as malaria and yellow fever.

Fast reactions!

Why is it so hard to swat a fly?
by Wanda

Like nearly all insects, flies have compound eyes—thousands of tiny lenses all looking at the same thing. That means flies can detect an object—like a swatter—the moment it starts moving toward them, and can dodge quickly out of the way.

Lens

Compound eye

Houseflies can't bite or chew, so they can only eat food in liquid form. Like humans, they have to mix solid foods with saliva before they can eat them.

A housefly vomits its stomach juices onto food to turn it into a liquid. Then the fly slurps it all up. Yuck!

The Praying Mantis

Under threat, a praying mantis rises up on its back legs and stretches its front legs to make itself look as big as possible.

Spikes on the front legs stick into prey to stop it from escaping.

Praying mantises are fierce hunters. They wait for smaller insects and ambush them with lightning speed. A mantis grabs its prey in its huge front legs—which are folded into massive pincers—and then bites off its head. The mantis has large eyes to spot prey, and it can swivel its head around to see behind it.

Different mantis species have different colors. They often choose to camouflage themselves in locations where they blend in with the environment.

Creepy!

While waiting for its next victim, a mantis holds its front legs up in front of its head, like it's praying in church. That's how it got its name.

Are mantises cannibals?
by Arnold

A cannibal is an animal that eats others of its own kind. Scientists watching mantises, both in captivity and in the wild, have seen female mantises kill males after mating. In some cases, the female will also eat him! Not all species of praying mantis are cannibalistic, but in those that are, cannibalism happens pretty often.

Cockroaches

Frizzle Fact

A cockroach can survive for a month without food and for a week without its head!

A cockroach can eat almost any food. In homes, it can survive on scraps of food, grease, and even soap and glue!

One insect no one likes to see is the cockroach. In the wild, cockroaches eat rotting wood, dung, and fungus, but they are also found in homes. The roaches stay out of sight during the day, but come out at night to search for scraps of food.

Pesky pest!

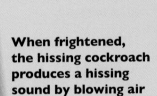

What makes an insect a pest?
by Dorothy Ann

Roaches have spread all over the world in the last few hundred years. They like warm places to live that are not too dry, so a human home is perfect. Without predators, their numbers keep growing, and that's when they start to cause problems. Insects become pests when too many of them enter houses or eat crops.

When frightened, the hissing cockroach produces a hissing sound by blowing air out of its abdomen.

Yum! That's my kind of snack!

Female roaches carry their eggs in a case that sticks out of the back of the abdomen. They lay the case and the eggs hatch when the baby cockroaches are big enough.

Egg case

Whizzing Dragonflies

Dragonflies are some of the fastest insect fliers in the world. They are hunters—they use their speed to chase other insects through the air. They swoop down to grab prey from the surface of water or nearby plants.

Dragonflies start life underwater. They grab small insects to eat with their spearlike jaws.

Like dragonflies, damselflies live and hunt near slow-moving water, such as ponds and lakes.

Unlike dragonflies, damselflies fold their wings back against their bodies.

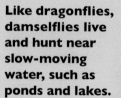

Frizzle Fact

About 300 million years ago, there was a giant dragonfly with wings 2 feet (60 centimeters) across.

A dragonfly has four narrow wings and a long, slender abdomen. It also has huge eyes for tracking fast-moving prey.

Total control!

How do dragonflies fly?
by Tim

Dragonflies are truly amazing fliers. They can fly in all directions, including backward. They can even hover in one place, just like a helicopter. Their wings beat 30 times a second. When high-speed cameras are used to slow down a dragonfly's movements, they show the secret to their flying skills—all four wings moving at their own speed and in different directions.

Defense Tactics

This walking stick's body looks like a twig. It sways in the breeze and fools predators.

Insects have to defend themselves against attack. Many of them use camouflage to stay out of sight. Others dash away to avoid getting trapped. Some insects fight back with bites and stings. Ms. Frizzle showed us a bombardier beetle. It got ready to attack the school bus with a spray of scalding liquid! "Quick! Time to head back to class," said the Friz.

Watch out! The bombardier can aim its spray in any direction.

Frizzle Fact

When attacked by ants, some termites explode, covering the ants in sticky goo. The goo tangles up the ants, giving the rest of the termites time to escape.

Hide-and-seek!

Spray gun
A mixture of liquids pumped into the tip of the beetle's abdomen creates a tiny explosion. It sends out a spray of hot gas and liquid.

How does camouflage work?
by Phoebe

Camouflage is when an insect uses patterns and colors to make its body look like something else. Some copy the colors of their surroundings to blend in unnoticed. Others disguise themselves as objects, such as leaves, flowers, or twigs. Many harmless insects look like more dangerous insects. For example, a hoverfly has black and yellow stripes that make it look like a bee or wasp. This is called mimicry, and it helps keep predators away.

A bombardier beetle sprays any attacker that touches it. A predator that manages to get the beetle in its mouth will soon spit it out.

Amazing Insects

Ant lion

Adult ant lions are flimsy flying insects that couldn't harm a fly—or any other insect. However, their larvae are much tougher. They dig pits in sand and bury themselves in the middle. When an ant falls in and can't climb up the sandy slope, the ant lion larva snaps it up in its jaws.

Dobsonfly

These flying insects have large mouthparts. The males have the biggest, although they do not use them to bite. Instead they use their mouthparts to grab hold of a female during mating. The female (pictured) can give a nasty bite. You can see dobsonflies around ponds and lakes. The larvae live underwater hunting other insects.

Cow killer

This is a wasp, although only the males have wings. The wingless females have a very powerful sting. Old-timers say the sting is bad enough to kill a cow. It isn't really, but the sting is very painful. Cow Killers live alone, not in nests, and are found in dry parts of North America.

Earwig

Earwigs have long pincers sticking out from their abdomens. They use them for fighting and for grabbing hold of food. The name earwig comes from the Old English word for "ear insect," and probably comes from the shape of the insect's wings—when outstretched, they look a bit like ears.

Well done, class! Let's get ready for our next adventure!

Giant weta

This huge cricket lives in New Zealand. The Maori people named it after the god of ugly things. Wetas are too heavy to fly and have no wings. They chew on leaves and fruits and fight off attackers by waving their long, spiky back legs at them.

Tiger beetle

Tiger beetles are fast predators that chase ants and other prey across the ground before grabbing them in their big, pincer-like mouthparts. These colorful beetles run so fast their eyes cannot see properly. They often bump into things because they can't see them in time.

Water strider

These bugs are found on the surface of still water. They scoot around on the surface, grabbing insects that have fallen into the water and can't get out. Their long legs spread their weight to stop them from sinking — they will drown if they go under. Their feet are covered in hairs that keep them dry.

Stalk-eyed fly

These flies have an eye at the end of a long stalk that grows out of either side of the head. When it's time to mate, the males stand on a branch to show off their eye stalks. To find out who the top fly is, they line up their eyes to see whose head is the widest.

29

Working with Insects

There are a million species, or types, of insects, so there is a lot to learn about them. Although insects are very rare in the ocean, they are found just about everywhere on land. Even though insects are small and can be hard to see, they play an important role in wildlife communities.

These "rocks" are termite nests. This entomologist is studying the insects that live inside them.

❮ Entomologist

A scientist who studies insects is called an entomologist. These scientists examine insects from the wild to see how they evolve and to find out how they live with all the other plants and animals in an area. It is important to understand what each insect species does in the habitat in which they live. If that habitat is damaged by human activity, entomologists can help fix it.

⌃ Beekeeper

Beekeepers look after honeybees. They give the bees a place to live inside a specially built box called a hive. The bees make honey in the hive, which the beekeeper collects every few weeks. Honey is sweet and good to eat.

All the honey we eat is collected this way. However, honeybees do more than just make honey. They travel around collecting nectar and pollen from all kinds of plants. As they move from flower to flower, the bees transfer pollen, which the plants need to produce seeds. Without honeybees and other flower-feeding insects, many important fruits and crops wouldn't be able to produce seeds and keep growing year after year.

❯ Farmer

A farmer is someone who grows crops or keeps livestock to sell for food. Some insects are pests that attack a farmer's crops, which means the farm produces smaller harvests. Some farmers get help from other insects that prey on the pests. Farmers leave patches of natural plants among their crops to make sure that the useful insects have a safe place to live.

Words to Know

Antenna A feeler on the head of an insect.

Camouflage A natural coloring that allows animals to hide by making them look like their surroundings.

Captivity The condition of being held by humans and not living in the wild.

Environment The natural surroundings of living things, such as the air, land, or sea.

Evolve To change slowly and naturally over time.

Honeycomb A wax structure made by bees to store honey and pollen.

Larva An insect at the stage of development between an egg and a pupa, when it looks like a worm.

Maggot The larva of certain flies that looks like small worms. It often feeds on rotting animal flesh.

Mate The male or female partner of a pair of animals. They join together to produce babies. This is called mating.

Nectar A sweet liquid from flowers that bees gather and make into honey.

Nymph A young form of an insect, such as a grasshopper, that changes into an adult by shedding its skin many times.

Oxygen A colorless gas found in the air and in water. Humans and most animals need oxygen to live.

Pollen Tiny grains produced in the anthers of flowers.

Predator An animal that hunts other animals for food.

Prey An animal that is hunted by another animal for food.

Stealthy Acting with or characterized by silence, secrecy, and caution.

Stinger A sharp, pointed part of an insect that can be used to sting.

Termite An insect like an ant that eats wood. Termites build large mounds, where they live in colonies.

Venom Poison produced by some animals, including insects. Venom is usually passed into a victim's body through a bite or sting.